A Dorling Kindersley Book

Project Editor Linda Martin
Art Editors Anita Ruddell and Peter Bailey
Photography Pete Gardner

First published in Great Britain in 1991 by
Dorling Kindersley Publishers Limited,
9 Henrietta Street, London WC2E 8PS
Reprinted 1992, 1993

A CIP catalogue record for this book is available
from the British Library.

ISBN 0-86318-509-6

Reproduced in Hong Kong by Bright Arts
Typeset by Windsorgraphics, Ringwood, Hampshire
Printed in Belgium

MY SCIENCE BOOK OF LIGHT

Written by
Neil Ardley

Dorling Kindersley • London

What is light ?

Imagine a world without light! It is not a pleasant thought, is it? Apart from making the world we live in bright and light, the light we receive from the Sun is essential for all life on Earth. Plants need light to grow, and animals and people feed on plants, or on the animals that eat plants. Although you cannot see light "moving", rays from the Sun travel at fantastic speed – almost 300,000 kilometres (186,300 miles) per second! In fact, nothing travels faster than light.

Broken straws?
Light rays change direction as they leave water. This "bending" of the light rays makes these straws look bent in the middle, but they are actually straight.

Smile please!
Light from the camera's flash travels to the object or person being photographed. It bounces off the subject, travels back to enter the camera lens, and forms an image of the subject on the film.

Sinister shadows
Shadows form because light rays can only travel in straight lines. Because rays do not bend around objects, shadows have the same shape as the objects.

Studying the stars
Astronomers use telescopes to learn about distant stars. The stars are so far away that their light takes many years to travel here.

Glowing in the dark
Some fish that live deep in the sea make their own light. It is so dark that they glow in order to see one another.

⚠ This sign means **take care.** You should ask an adult to help you with this step of the experiment.

Be a safe scientist
Follow all the directions carefully and always take care, especially with glass, scissors, matches, candles, and electricity. Never put anything in your mouth or eyes. Never stare at the Sun or at any bright light as you could damage your eyes. Remember to switch off torches and electric lights after using them. Never touch electric light bulbs as they get very hot.

Shadow play

Why do shadows appear behind objects when light shines on them? Make a theatre in which the players are shadows. It will show you how light travels in straight rays and you will see how shadows form.

You will need:

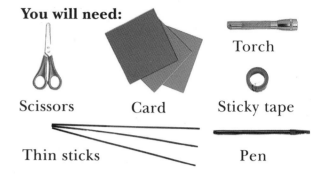

Scissors   Card   Torch   Sticky tape

Thin sticks   Pen

1 Draw a bird shape, or any shape you like, on the card.

2 Carefully cut around the shape. You may need an adult's help with this.

You may like to make a hole for the eye.

3 Tape your shape to the end of a thin stick.

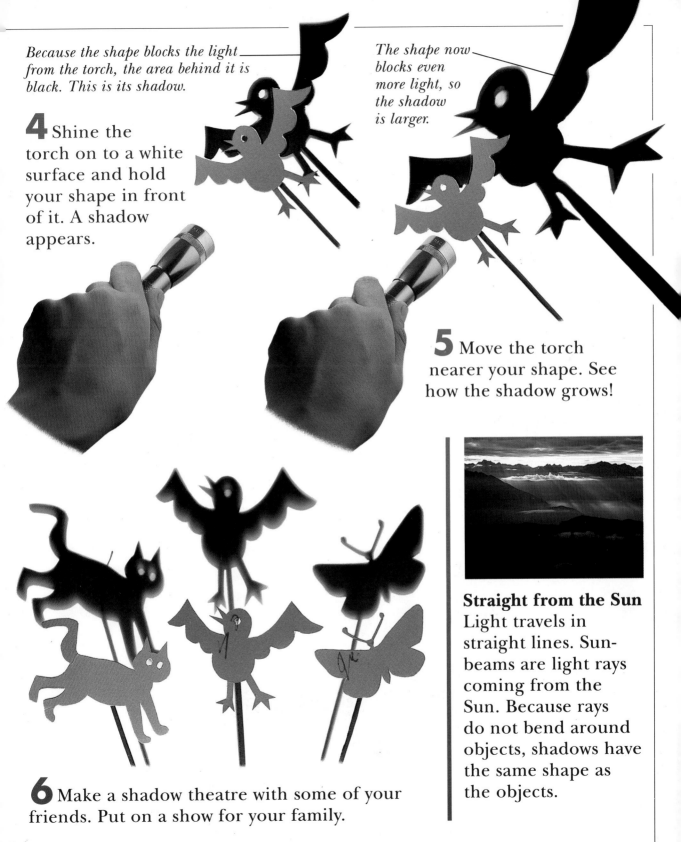

Because the shape blocks the light from the torch, the area behind it is black. This is its shadow.

The shape now blocks even more light, so the shadow is larger.

4 Shine the torch on to a white surface and hold your shape in front of it. A shadow appears.

5 Move the torch nearer your shape. See how the shadow grows!

6 Make a shadow theatre with some of your friends. Put on a show for your family.

Straight from the Sun
Light travels in straight lines. Sunbeams are light rays coming from the Sun. Because rays do not bend around objects, shadows have the same shape as the objects.

See around corners

Why can you see an image or reflection of something in a mirror? A flat, smooth surface like a mirror makes light rays bounce off, or "reflect" from it to form an image. Make a periscope and discover how mirrors can reflect light so that you can see around corners!

You will need:

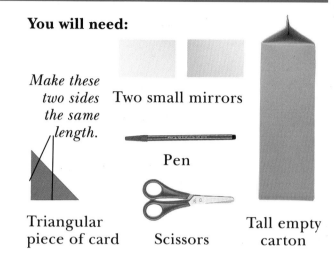

Make these two sides the same length.

Two small mirrors

Pen

Triangular piece of card

Scissors

Tall empty carton

1 Using the triangular piece of card, draw two diagonal lines on one side of the carton.

2 Cut a slot along each of the lines.

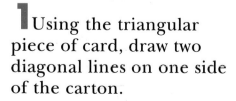

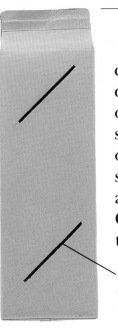

3 Turn the carton and draw two lines on the other side, directly opposite the slots you have already cut. Cut slots along these too.

Make sure the slots are in the same position on each side.

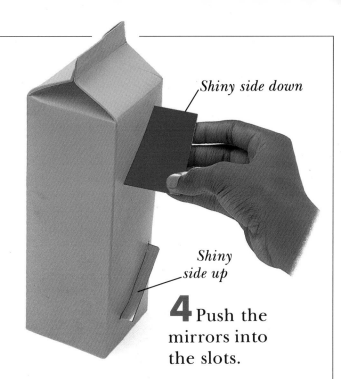

Shiny side down

Shiny side up

4 Push the mirrors into the slots.

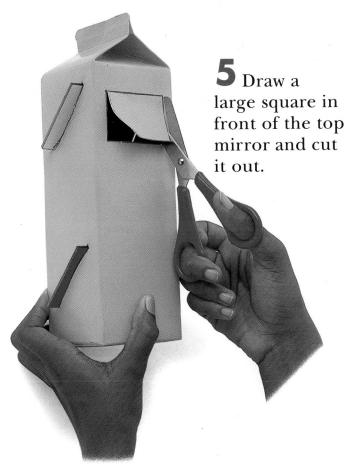

5 Draw a large square in front of the top mirror and cut it out.

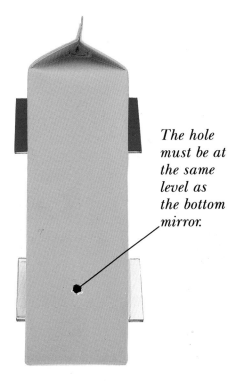

The hole must be at the same level as the bottom mirror.

6 With a pencil, make a small hole in the back of the carton. The periscope is now ready.

Continued on next page

7 You can use the periscope for looking around corners or over walls without being seen.

Light from the scene enters through the square at the front.

The top mirror sends this light to the bottom mirror.

The bottom mirror sends the light to your eye. You see an image of the scene.

Up periscope!

The crew of a submerged submarine uses a periscope to see what is happening at the surface of the sea. The periscope reflects light rays from the surface down a tube into the submarine. People also use periscopes to see above the heads of people in a crowd.

Continued from previous page

Pretty patterns

See how the light reflecting off three mirrors can form a beautiful pattern from just a few beads. Use the mirrors and beads to make a colourful kaleidoscope. Simply shake it to get a new pattern. You will find that you never get the same pattern twice!

You will need:

Three small mirrors

Pencil

Scissors

Torch

Card

Tracing paper

Sticky tape   Beads

1 Tape the mirrors together to form a triangle. You may need help to do this.

The shiny sides must be inside.

2 Stand the mirrors on the card and draw around the base.

Continued on next page

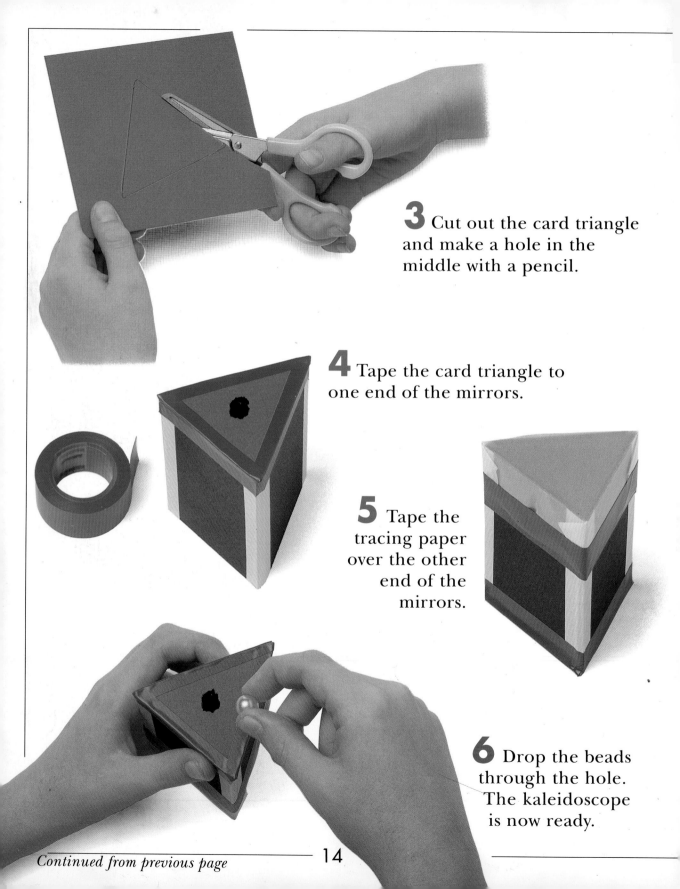

3 Cut out the card triangle and make a hole in the middle with a pencil.

4 Tape the card triangle to one end of the mirrors.

5 Tape the tracing paper over the other end of the mirrors.

6 Drop the beads through the hole. The kaleidoscope is now ready.

7 Shine the torch on the tracing paper and look through the hole. Move the kaleidoscope to change the pattern.

The pattern contains several images of the beads. Light rays bounce between the mirrors to form the images.

Power from the Sun

Nearly 2,000 mirrors catch the Sun's rays in this solar power station in California. The mirrors reflect the rays so that they all meet at a central tower, which turns the heat of the rays into electricity. The station produces enough electricity for a town of 20,000 people.

Light guide

Light normally travels in straight lines, but you can guide it along a curved tube. Guiding light in this way lets doctors see inside people to find out why they are ill.

You will need:

Black paper

Cardboard box

Lamp

Paint brush

Matt black paint

Sticky tape

Plasticine

Scissors

Short length of plastic tube

1 Paint the inside of the box with matt black paint. Leave it to dry.

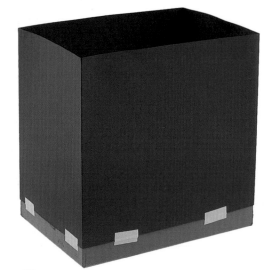

2 Cut the black paper and tape it around the outside of the box to make tall sides.

3 Make a hole in one end of the box and push the tube through. Leave the end of the tube sticking out.

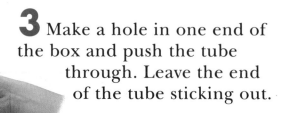

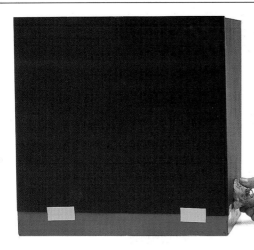

4 Stick plasticine around the tube on the outside of the box to stop light getting through the hole.

Light rays stay in the tube because they are bounced, or "reflected" from one side to the other as the light travels through the tube.

5 In a darkened room, shine the lamp on the end of the tube. Look into the box. See how the tube glows.

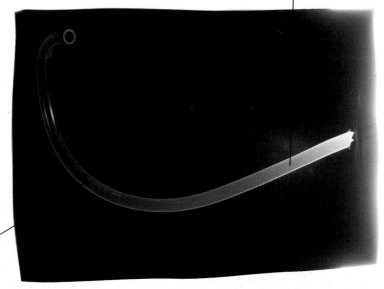

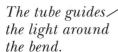

The tube guides the light around the bend.

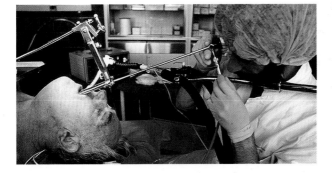

Inside view

Doctors can see inside people by using a tube that they put into the body. Light is guided along glass fibres in the tube to the doctor's eye. The doctor can then see an image of a part of the body.

Seeing double

Light travels in straight lines. Or does it? By doing these two simple experiments, you can find out how to make light bend, or "refract". Our eyes cannot tell that the light bends, and trick us into seeing things that appear to be impossible!

Pour the water carefully otherwise you may move the button.

1 Put the button in the glass. Make sure it is in the middle.

2 Gently pour some water into the glass. The button does not float.

3 Look at the glass from the side. An extra button has appeared, and it seems to float!

You see the button "floating" above the bottom of the glass.

The light rays change direction when they leave the water and make the straws look as if they bend in the middle.

4 Remove the button and put the straws into the glass of water. They seem to bend as they enter the water. Take the straws out. Nothing has happened to them!

Deep water

Pools and ponds are always deeper than they look. This is because the light rays from the bottom bend as they leave the water. This bending of the light makes the bottom of the pool or pond appear closer to us than it really is.

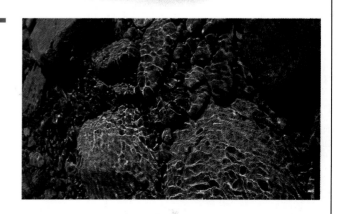

Bending light

Transparent materials bend, or "refract" light rays. By doing this experiment, you can show light beams bending as they pass through glass and water. You will see how the rays have to strike the glass at an angle in order to bend.

You will need:

 Sheet of white paper

Large cardboard box

Glass jar of water

Ruler

Pen

Torch

Scissors

1 Draw two lines, two centimetres apart, on one end of the box.

2 Cut narrow slits along both lines.

3 Put the sheet of paper in the bottom of the box.

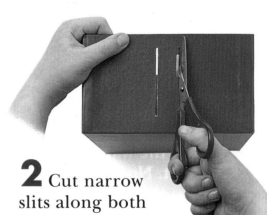

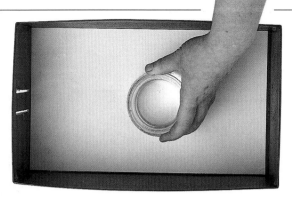

4 Carefully put the jar full of water in the box. Make sure you line the jar up with the two slits.

The light rays bend as they leave the jar.

The light rays change direction as they strike the curved surface of the jar at an angle.

5 In a darkened room, shine the torch through the two slits. See how the jar of water bends the light. You may need to move the jar until the rays meet.

The light is very bright where the rays meet.

Fire hazard
Glass can bend light rays from the sun. If the rays meet on some dry grass or wood, they can heat it so much that it bursts into flame. Never leave bottles or jars outside where they could start a fire!

Water magnifier

Use some water to make a simple magnifying lens. It will make small objects look larger. A magnifying lens bends, or "refracts" light rays coming from the objects to form an image that is bigger than the object itself.

You will need:

Jug of water

Large yoghurt pot

Plastic wrap

Rubber band

Small objects

1 Put the objects into the pot. Space them out evenly.

2 Cover the pot loosely with a piece of plastic wrap.

3 Secure the plastic wrap with the rubber band. Gently push the plastic wrap to make a small dip in it.

4 Carefully pour water into the dip.

The water is flat on top, but curved underneath. The curved surface makes the water into a lens.

Folds in the plastic wrap distort the objects at the side.

5 Look down into the pot. The water magnifies the objects.

The button looks much larger.

Magnifying glass

Some things are too small to see easily. A magnifying glass is a lens that makes objects look much bigger. The glass has curved sides that bend light rays passing through it. The bending forms a large image as you look into the glass.

Box camera

A magnifying glass can do more than make things look larger. You can use one to make a simple camera that can produce a picture.

You will need:

Tracing or tissue paper

Empty tissue box

Sticky tape

Magnifying glass

Cardboard tube

Pen

Scissors

1 Put the tube on the side of the box opposite the opening. Draw a circle around it.

2 Cut out the circle.

3 Gently push the tube into the hole you have just made. You should be able to move it in and out.

4 Tape the magnifying glass to the other end of the tube.

5 Tape the tracing paper over the opening in the box. The box camera is now ready.

6 Point the camera towards a brightly lit object. Look at the paper screen. An image of the object appears on the paper.

Move the tube in or out until the image is sharp.

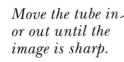

The magnifying glass bends light rays from the object to meet on the paper screen and form an image.

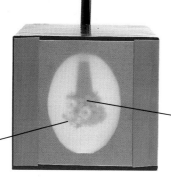

The image is upside down and back-to-front.

Taking photographs
A camera's lens is like the magnifying glass, but a camera has film in place of the tracing paper. The lens forms an image of a scene on the film. The photograph is developed and printed from the film.

Photo collection

Make a "photographic" picture of a whole collection of objects in just a few minutes. It should help you to understand how photography works.

You will need:

Box of photographic paper

Lamp

Black paper

Scissors

Pencil

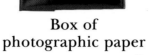

Small, flat objects

1 Draw some shapes on the black paper. Cut them out.

2 In a darkened room, take a piece of photographic paper out of its box. Quickly arrange the black paper and objects on the photographic paper.

3 Position the lamp over the paper. Switch it on and leave for about five minutes.

4 Switch off the lamp. Remove the black paper and all the objects. You now have a picture of the cut-out shapes and all the objects.

The paper becomes dark where the light reaches it.

The parts that were covered stay white.

5 The picture eventually begins to fade. The paper becomes dark all over as light can now reach every part of it.

Photo booth

In a photo booth, a lens forms images of you on a strip of photographic printing paper. A machine in the booth develops and fixes the pictures so that they form completely and do not fade.

Light for growth

All living things need light to live. Plants need light to grow. Without plants, all life on Earth would cease, as animals and people feed on plants, or on animals that eat plants.

You will need:

Jug of water

Paper towels

Box with lid

Scissors

Cress seeds

Sheet of plastic

Two pieces of card to fit inside box

1 Cut a large window in one end of the box.

2 Cut off one third of the box lid.

3 Put the plastic sheet and some paper towels in the box. Carefully add a little water.

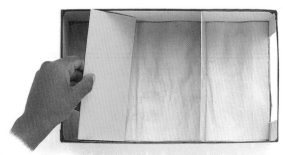

4 Divide the box into three sections with the two pieces of card.

5 Sprinkle some seeds into each section. Do this as evenly as you can.

6 Cover the window section and middle section with the lid. Face the window section towards the sun. The seeds will probably need watering daily.

The seedlings that have been open to the light grow normally.

The seedlings without light have started to grow, but are weak and will soon die.

These seedlings lean towards one side. They are growing towards the window to get light.

7 After about one week, take the lid off completely. The seedlings in the three sections are growing quite differently.

Picture credits
(Picture credits abbreviation key: B=below, C=centre, L=left, R=right, T=top)

Forestry Commission, Edinburgh: 21BL; Pete Gardner: 6TR, 6BL, 6BR, 7TL, 27BR; Malvin Van Gelderen: 25BL; The Image Bank: 7TR; NHPA/Agence Nature: 7CL; Royal Navy Submarine Museum:
12BR; Science Photo Library/ Simon Fraser: 9CR; Peter Menzel: 15BR; Philippe Plailly: 17BL; Clive Streeter: 23BR; Zefa: 19BR

Picture Research Kate Fox

Title page photography Dave King

Dorling Kindersley would like to thank Claire Gillard for editorial
assistance and Mark Regardsoe for design assistance; Mrs Bradbury, the staff and children of Allfarthing Junior School, Wandsworth, especially Joe Armstrong, Mark Baker, Melanie Best, Edward Dormer, Karen Masterson, Dorothy Opong, Felix Scott, Natasha Shepherd, Alice Watling and Anton Whitelocke.

Hinduism

Anita Ganeri

QED Publishing

Copyright © QED Publishing 2006

First published in the UK in 2006 by
QED Publishing
A Quarto Group company
226 City Road
London EC1V 2TT
www.qed-publishing.co.uk

A catalogue record for this book is available from the British Library.

ISBN 1 84538 385 0

Written by Anita Ganeri
Designed by Tall Tree Books
Editor Louisa Somerville
Consultant John Keast

Publisher Steve Evans
Creative Director Zeta Davies
Editorial Director Jean Coppendale

Printed and bound in China

Picture credits To follow

Key: t = top, b = bottom, c = centre, l = left, r = right, FC = front cover

Ark Religion /Helene Rogers 5t 5b, 7t, 8t 8b, 9t, 11t 11b, 12, 13t 13b, 14, 16, 21b, 25b, 27b /Peter Rauter title page, 24 /Robin Graham 4; **Dinodia Photo Library** 6, 10, 21t, 25t /Fiona Good 7b, 15b, 17t, 20, 23t /Andrea Alborno 15t; **Trip** 22 /Adina Tovey 26 /Robin Smith 27t.

Website information is correct at the time of going to press.
However, the publishers cannot accept liability for any information
or links found on third-party websites.

Words in **bold** are explained
in the glossary on page 30.